Every King Needs a Queen, Not a Handmaiden:

A Bird's Eye View from a Woman's Perspective

Jayne Okonji

Every King Needs a Queen, Not a Handmaiden: A Bird's Eye View from a Woman's Perspective
Copyright © Jayne Okonji, 2019

Dedication

To all the queens and potential queens out there who inspired me to write this book; keep showing up, God has got your back. You rock!!!

And to all the real kings out there; you sure make the world go round.

About the Author

Jayne Okonji is a charismatic young lady and an aspiring entrepreneur. She attended and graduated from the world renowned Covenant University in Nigeria with a BSc in Economics. She proceeded to get her MBA from University of Houston–Clear Lake. She is married to Philip Okonji, and they are blessed with three beautiful girls Ogechuka, Kachiku, and Chizite. She is the CEO/Consultant of Jayberek Management and Consulting Services, which specializes in providing consulting services for Home Healthcare services and currently works as a manager with a healthcare company.

Jayne Okonji
2019

Contents

The Purpose of the Book

While growing up as a young lady, I had observed a problem that boggled my mind, because I could not understand why it was so. However, now as a married adult and after critical analysis, observations, and discussions with others, I have come to realize a major cause of the problem: The problem is as a result of a wrong mindset. I had in the past passionately discussed the problem with others, sharing my thoughts, insights, and frustrations; but after pondering for a while, I decided not to just talk about the issue in my personal space but to write about it on a broader scale in order to enlighten other people and to help change the "mindset" behind this problem.

It is a mindset in which a lot of wives are regarded and treated as being inferior or less than their husbands, and their husbands are regarded as their "bosses." Moreover, their husbands feel they have a right to treat their wives as inferior to them, and the level of their manliness is judged based on how much they "lord" it over their wives. It is also a mindset that subjects wives most times to a life of servitude and suffering with little or no help from their husbands.

There have been a number of teachings, admonishing wives to regard, honor, and treat their husbands like "kings" in their home. And I agree with this premise, but I do not think this teaching is balanced without acknowledging that a "king" (husband) is not complete without a "queen" (wife). A king is not usually matched with a handmaiden but with a queen. Moreover, even if a king marries a handmaiden, she gets a status change and immediately becomes a queen. Esther, a slave girl, was immediately made queen as soon as the king chose her in Esther 2:17. So with this background laid, let me elaborate further on my perspective, which will be in the context of Christian marriage.

Chapter One
Definition of Terms

~⟨♡⟩~

1 Who Is a King?

According to the Merriam-Webster dictionary, a king is a male monarch of a major territorial unit, a paramount chief, or one that holds a preeminent position.

As stated above, a king is a leader of a territorial unit; and so relating this concept to the family unit, I will liken the husband (man) to the "king" in the household, as he is the leader in the home or the head of the family. He holds a preeminent role as the head or leader of the family. His role in the family unit is vital, and a family unit without its head would be incomplete or lacking in some form. Of course, this does not mean that single-parent family units cannot thrive; however, they would thrive even greater if there was a "king" in the picture.

Therefore, in the context of the husband being the "king," who then is a "queen"?

2 Who Is a Queen?

Of course, there are several definitions for a queen according to the dictionary, but in the context of our discussion we will define a queen as the wife of a king (Merriam-Webster dictionary). A queen is very important and complements the king, meaning that a king is not complete without a queen by his side, or as it is popularly said: "Beside every successful man, there is a great woman."

Moreover, a queen usually enjoys the social rank and status of her husband. In the context of our "royal" metaphor, we must consider the definition of a handmaiden.

3 Who Is a Handmaiden?

According to the Merriam-Webster dictionary, a *handmaiden* is a personal maid or female servant or something whose essential function is to serve or assist. A handmaiden may be of slave status or may be an employee. However, in the context of our discussion, the term handmaiden explicitly implies to a lower class or an inferior status, whose main duties is to serve and assist the master.

4 Biblical Mention of Handmaiden

In the Bible, the term *handmaiden* describes a female slave who served her mistress. In the case of Abraham and Sarai, Hagar is described as Sarai's handmaid (Genesis 16:1); likewise, Zilpah was Leah's handmaid (Genesis 29:24), and Bilhah was Rachel's handmaid (Genesis 29:29). In each of these cases, the mistress "gave" her handmaid to her husband solely to bear children for him. In these cases, the handmaiden's role was to give "seed" to her mistress, and they were of no real importance beyond that role. The position of a handmaid was one of humility and respectful submission in the presence of her owners and masters.

Now that we have established the various definitions described above, let us discuss what marriage is and what the role of a wife/queen is as it relates to her husband in a marriage relationship.

5 What Is Marriage?

Before we go further, let us look at what marriage is and the reason God instituted it. Marriage, in the most simplistic term according to Genesis 2:24, is the union (spiritually, physically, and emotionally) of two flesh —male and female to become one flesh.

According to Genesis 2:18, the Lord God said, "It is not good that man should be alone; I will make him a helper comparable to him" (NKJV). God had given Man the responsibility to be fruitful, multiply, subdue, replenish, and have dominion over the earth and over everything He had created as evidenced in Genesis 1:26–28:

> Let Us make man in Our image, according to Our likeness; let them have dominion over the fish of the sea, over the birds of the air, and over the cattle, over all the earth and over every creeping thing that creeps on the earth." So God created man in His own image; in the image of God He created him; male and female He created them. Then God blessed them, and God said to them, "Be fruitful and multiply; fill the earth and subdue it; have dominion over the fish of the sea, over the birds of the air, and over every living thing that moves on the earth" (NKJV).

The responsibility God had given Adam was a huge one; thus, God considered that Adam would need some help to accomplish it. So God made him a helper (a wife), who meets his needs and complements him; so, both of them, as a team, can accomplish God's will for them.

As indicated in the passage above, the woman (wife) was to be a helper. Therefore, if she was supposed to be a helper, then let us explore who a helper is and the helper's role in the marriage relationship.

6 *The Concept of Help*

The general concept of the word *help* means to give assistance or support to; that is, to make it easier for someone to do something by offering one's services or resources. This means to voluntarily lend a helping hand to someone or to come to the aid of someone.

According to the Bible, the term *helper* or *helpmeet* comes from the Hebrew words *ezer kenegdo—ezer* is a combination of two meanings, "to rescue/save" and "to be strong"; and the word *kenegdo* means "opposite as to him" or "corresponding as to him." Thus relating this definition to our discussion, a wife is an equal and uniquely created individual to her husband, she provides a complementary and perfect fit to the husband, she is a strong rescue and strength for the man (husband). Every man has a destiny to fulfill; and if he adequately works in unity with his "helper" (wife)—who can help strengthen and save or rescue him—she would make his life much easier and he would experience a greater fulfillment of purpose.

I like the way Jimena describes the role of the man and woman in her blog (*Ezer Kenegdo*),[1] she describes the man and woman like two hands. Your left hand and right hand are in ways the same but also different. You have bones, muscles, veins, skin, nails. And you have fingers and a thumb on each hand. Your left and right hand are the exact opposite of each other, but the one hand is not more important than the other one. One hand might be a little stronger and is your preferred hand, but you can perfectly use each hand on its own. Together your hands can do more. They are even stronger than your preferred hand. You can get more done with less effort when using both hands together. Of course this is only going to work when your one hand is the *kenegdo* to your other hand.

So in analyzing the concept of a *helper* as it relates to the woman, we can see that the reason God introduced Eve to Adam was for the purpose of providing companionship ("It is not good for the man to be alone" [Genesis 2:18, NIV].) and to be a helper (*ezer kenegdo*). Now the "helper" (wife) who was introduced into the scene does not eliminate the role of the one who needs help (that is, the husband); nor does it make the husband fold his hands while the one who was given to "help" is made to take on both parties' roles.

---

1 Cited from the article entitled "Ezer Kenegdo" found at <https://ezerkenegdo. org/ezer-kenegdo/>, February 22, 2018.

Chapter Two
God's Design for Marriage

~❦~

7 God's Structure for Marriage

In the New Testament, God gave a structure after which the marriage relationship should be patterned. Let us look more closely at this relationship in Ephesians 5: 21–33:

> Out of respect for Christ, be courteously reverent to one another.
>
> Wives, understand and support your husbands in ways that show your support for Christ. The husband provides leadership to his wife the way Christ does to his church, not by domineering but by cherishing. So just as the church submits to Christ as he exercises such leadership, wives should likewise submit to their husbands.
>
> Husbands, go all out in your love for your wives, exactly as Christ did for the church—a love marked by giving, not getting. Christ's love makes the church whole. His words evoke her beauty. Everything he does and says is designed to bring the best out of her, dressing her in dazzling white silk, radiant with holiness. And that is how husbands ought to love their wives. They're really doing themselves a favor—since they're already "one" in marriage.
>
> No one abuses his own body, does he? No, he feeds and pampers it. That's how Christ treats us, the church, since we are part of his body. And this is why a man leaves father and mother and cherishes his wife. No longer two, they become "one flesh." This is a huge mystery, and I don't pretend to understand it all. What is clearest to me is the way Christ treats the church. And this provides a good picture of how each husband is to treat his wife, loving himself in loving her, and how each wife is to honor her husband (MSG).

In the above verses, we can see that the wife's submission to her husband is in relationship with how the Church submits to Christ's leadership, and the leadership to be displayed by the husband is in relation to Jesus' leadership of the Church. Since Jesus' leadership is the example the Bible gives of a man's leadership in marriage, then let us explore Jesus' leadership of the Church.

8 Loving as Christ Loved

Ephesians 5 requires the husband to exercise and model his leadership of his wife by loving her, just as Christ loved the Church and gave himself up for her (Church).

This passage also states that "husbands ought to love their wives as their own bodies" (verse 28). Since the husband loves his body by nourishing and cherishing it, then in loving his wife, he should likewise nourish and cherish his wife as he does his own body.

In a loving husband's leadership role as the head, he leads by giving of himself to his wife just like Christ gave Himself for His Bride (the Church). Christ's giving of Himself was personal and sacrificial. This principle of self-giving sets the standard for all the ways in which a man's love can be unselfishly manifested and realized.

Christ's giving of Himself is for the benefit of His Bride (Church) in order "to make her holy, cleansing her by the washing with water through the word, and to present her to himself as a radiant church" (Ephesians 5:26–27, NIV). Therefore, a husband's love is to be beneficial to the wife, just as Christ's love is beneficial to the Church. It should be a love that is characterized by the giving of oneself for the benefit of the other party so that the marriage can be beautiful and enjoyed. Moreover, just as Christ works to present His Church to Himself as His glorious bride, the husband ought to work to make his wife and their marriage glorious.

However, let me add a caveat here by saying, a husband cannot truly love his wife without first loving himself, because a person cannot give out what they do not have. If you do not have love for yourself, then you cannot love someone else, and you do not have the capacity to love someone else because you hate yourself. If you encounter a husband that mistreats, beats or hates his wife, it usually is a clear indication that he does not love himself, because he can only treat her as good as he treats himself. So admonishing a husband to love his wife like he loves his own body will not apply to a husband who hates himself. That husband will first need to seek his identity and love for himself from God and allow God to help him love himself first before he can love anyone else.

Chapter Three
Wrong Mentality,
Wrong Outcome

Over the years, I have seen and heard of so many stories in which women have been treated like handmaidens and like they were inferior to their spouses and not like queens, as they ought to be treated. I call it the "handmaiden wife" mentality. In this chapter, we will explore some true-life stories of some of these women who have been treated like handmaidens and not like queens.

There are so many more sad stories that cannot all be recounted in this book. Since a lot of these stories would be somewhat similar to other women's experiences, a lot of women will be able to relate to them. Now in most of these cases, the husbands are not necessarily the problem, but it is the mindset of the husband that is the problem.

The purpose of this book is not to portray marriage in a bad light or portray husbands as the villains that are heartless and hate their wives. But the purpose is to highlight some of the sufferings and relegations women have had to endure because of this wrong mindset, which has been perpetuated from one generation to the next. Another purpose is to show how a husband—not being intentional, or taking seemingly little things for granted—can be perceived as being uncaring and insensitive. I believe a husband with a better understanding of his wife's worth and value will treat her even more graciously.

9 True Life Stories

A lot of these true life stories are centered around household chores, finances, fidelity, and sex because these are some of the major sources of conflict that expose the wrong mentality this book seeks to address.

Story 1

There is a story told of a newly married couple in which the wife just had a baby, but the husband was so busy with his career and building his "empire" that he barely paid any attention to his new family. The new wife could not get her husband to communicate or interact with her or the new baby when he returned home from work. Instead, he would rather demand for his meal and for his personal needs be met, while largely neglecting his wife.

My Analysis:

A lot of wives might have experienced something somewhat similar to this story at one point or another in their marriage, in which the husband is working hard to provide for the family and to be successful—but often at the detriment of his family relationships. A woman is an emotional and intellectual person that needs to be interacted with, not ignored or overlooked. A wife earnestly desires to communicate with her husband because this tells her that she is important to him. She is not meant to be merely a "decoration trophy" in the home in order to show that a woman is present or just meant to meet her husband's needs.

My mentor Bishop T. D. Jakes once explained that the art of balancing work, leisure, and family life is like a juggler (this is the skill of keeping several objects in motion in the air at the same time by alternately tossing and catching them). The juggler does not hold on to anyone object too long at the expense of the other objects, otherwise the other objects he is juggling will fall to the ground. It is a fine art mastered over time. Thus, relating the art of juggling to balancing work, family, and leisure, one aspect of person's life should not get all the attention at the detriment of the other aspects of that person's life; this will not lead to balance and fulfillment in life.

Therefore, a husband who has excess leisure time or family time is most likely a "broke" husband or father; and a husband who works too much all the time will most likely be an "absentee" husband or father. So a husband needs to learn the fine art of balancing all the aspects of his life, so that just like the juggler's tossed objects, no aspect of his life fails or suffers neglect.

Sadly, some workaholics do not know when work is too much work. However, their wives and kids can serve as a guard rail when they are going overboard, if they humbly receive their feedback. Regrettably, some laid-back men do not know when there is too much idling; but their families' financial state and wellbeing should serve as a wake up call.

Story 2

There is another story of a husband whose wife had gone to the hospital to give birth to their child. Yet, while she was in the hospital giving birth and then recovering from childbirth, neither the husband nor the children attended to the house chores. Instead, all the dirty laundry and dishes that the kids and the husband had accumulated during her hospital stay were left undone, and they were waiting for her to do them when she returned home.

There are two other related stories in which the pregnant wives could not do the family laundry because they had fallen very sick in the course of their pregnancy. In the first case, the husband selected his clothes from the pile of laundry and only washed his own laundry, while leaving his pregnant wife's and his children's dirty laundry, even though the wife before she got sick had always been the one doing the family's laundry, including the husband's laundry.

In the second case, the wife's soaked laundry was neglected by the spouse even though the wife was sick and could not do it. The clothes ended up getting ruined and had to be discarded. When the wife asked her husband why he did not help her with the soaked laundry, he told her it was not his duty to wash their soaked laundry or the wife's laundry, but it was the wife's duty to wash the husband's clothes, notwithstanding that she had always been the one doing all of their laundry in the past.

My Analysis:

A wife is not to be seen as a handmaiden/slave whose sole duty is to meet her husband's and family's needs. She is a special royalty and should be seen and treated as such, and not solely reduced to a housekeeper. Going through childbirth is emotionally taxing; it is a strenuous and painful experience and going through that experience without the adequate support of a spouse is even more traumatic and heartbreaking. Imagine how bad the wife would have felt knowing that she could not count on her husband's help at a time she needed it most. The husband could have easily washed the clothes and dishes for his wife, but he had the "handmaiden wife" mindset—that it was solely his wife's duty to do all these chores—which kept him from helping her out when he could, even at a crucial time of childbirth when she needed all the help and support she could get.

In the second scenario, it is particularly disheartening that the first husband would select and wash only his laundry even though his wife had always washed all of the family's clothes; but when she was unable to get the laundry done, she could not count on her husband's help. It is also sad that the second husband had the mindset that it was not his duty to help his wife with her laundry, but it was the wife's duty to help him with his. Now in both scenarios, the "handmaiden wife" mentality is clearly evident. So even though the husbands were available and able to help their sick and pregnant wives, they did not because they had the mindset that it is the duty of the wives and not theirs, which is a sad mentality that is at work here.

The wives in these stories decided after the incident to stop doing their husband's laundry, and I do not believe anyone should fault them at all. It is not okay for the wives to help their husbands with their chores, but the husband in turn thinks it is demeaning or belittling to help their wives with theirs, especially when they are sick or unable to do their chores.

Story 3

Another story is told of a wife who was cooking a meal for the husband (and, by the way, she had to cook a new meal every day because the husband could not eat day-old food), and their baby had soiled his diaper, and the husband called the wife to "take a break" from cooking to come change the baby's diaper. And after she was done cleaning the baby, she had to go back to the kitchen and resume cooking, while he sat in the living room watching his television program the whole time!

My Analysis:

Now the question one might ask is: if the man was by himself, would he cook a new meal for himself every day? Or, is it because he has someone, namely his wife, whom he thinks should meet his every need that he chooses to make a selfish demand on her, whether or not she feels up to it or not?

If she still goes ahead to do his bidding like the submissive wife she is expected to be, then would it be too much for him to help by changing the baby's diaper while she cooks a fresh meal for him? But instead, he had to call her to "take a break" from cooking and clean the baby up and then go back and resume her cooking while he sits watching TV. You can see the "handmaiden wife" mindset on display here; his wife is nothing more than his handmaiden, and she is expected to do all the household chores and meet all his needs, while he is barely giving anything back in return. Some could argue that he was too tired after a hard day's work, but that excuse does not hold because it does not take a lot of energy to change a baby's soiled diaper. Moreover, the baby needs his father's interaction and loving care, too.

Story 4

Another sad story is told of a husband whose wife was very sick and in a lot of pain. She begged her husband to help her make a simple meal, but instead he set a pot of water on the stove and then asked his wife to get up to make the meal herself. Even though all through their marriage, she had always been the one cooking and serving her husband. However, when she needed him to do the same for her just one time, he could not bring himself to do the same for her.

My analysis:

If the wife was her husband's "queen" and he cared deeply for her, it should not be a big deal to help, especially when she was sick and needed help (keeping in mind that she had always cooked for him). Some may argue that he might not know how to make the meal she requested, but this was not the case because he knew how to make the meal. Nevertheless, if he did not know how to make it, he could have asked her for directions or attempted to make the meal on his own, even if it would not come out perfectly. After all, a sick person will most likely not be worried about the food being perfect.

Story 5

There is another story told of a wife who could not eat with her husband from the same plate. This meant that after she dished the food for both of them, she would not eat with him until he was done eating; then she would get to eat what was leftover.

My Analysis:

Now in this story, if it was the husband that ordered the wife not to eat with him, then I think the wife could have served their meal separately instead of serving both their meals together and then waiting to eat what he had left over of their meal. Of course, if it was her personal decision not to eat from the same plate with him, then that is a "lowly" mentality the wife is displaying and not one of respect or reverence for her husband.

Let us further analyze the mentality at play here. First, if it was the man that requested she should not eat from the same plate with him, then that feeds the narrative of a wife being seen as inferior to her husband and so is not worthy to eat from the same plate as her husband. It is just like a master who does not expect his hired servant to eat at his table, not to mention eating from his master's plate. In a marriage relationship, however, God did not design marriage to be a master/servant relationship. Instead, it should be a king-queen relationship in which both husband and wife respect, honor, and cherish each other deeply. Neither of the parties should be inferior to the other. Some would argue that the wife's action is a sign of honor and respect for her husband—until he is done eating, she should not eat from the same plate with him. However, I believe that is an oppressive and archaic way to think. Even Jesus, the King of kings, sat at the table and ate and broke bread with his disciples; and the husband here is not greater than Jesus.

Story 6

Another story was told of a husband who demanded for his wife to kneel and greet him as her "lord" every day, with all the required adulation and genuflection. If she failed to do so, then she would not be given any allowance for food or upkeep of the home; and sometimes, she was even beaten.

My Analysis:

Now there is nothing wrong if a woman desires of her own free will to greet her husband with all the praises and genuflections she desires. It is a good thing. However, when the greeting is coerced and used as a means of manipulation, then that is wrong. One might ask why she is not fending for herself and has to depend on her husband; but in some parts of the world, especially in West Africa, the husband sometimes requires the wife to be a housewife and take care of the children, especially when the husband is rich and can exclusively support the family financially.

So imagine a situation in which the wife is solely dependent on the husband financially and would need to meet some strict obligations to enjoy any financial benefits, then that is a major manipulative "power play" at work. In this case, money is used as a "power tool" by the husband to coerce and manipulate his wife. A woman ought to be pampered and taken care of financially, especially when the husband has the financial means—without using his resources as a means for manipulating and suppressing his spouse as he pleases. A husband's "queen" should not be reduced to a handmaiden that has to greet her master in his own specific way for it to be accepted.

Story 7

Another story is told of a husband who made daily demands of sex from his wife. Whenever she indicated she was too tired and could not meet his sexual needs, he would instantly start acting maliciously toward her and would withhold money for upkeep of the house. He did not empathize with the hardships she faced because of her financial dependence on him. And at times, he would even beat her when she refused.

My Analysis:

As I referenced in story six above, in some families the wife is expected to be a housewife and take care of the home and the children, especially when the husband is rich. However, in this case, it became a means of control. So a beautiful act such as sexual intercourse—which ought to be enjoyed by both parties—becomes a chore and duty that must be performed daily by the wife. If not, she would suffer some unpleasant consequences.

A wife is not a sex slave (handmaiden) who must be available whenever her husband needs her. She has a right to respectfully and kindly turn down her husband's advances when she is not in the mood or not able to. Moreover, that should not earn her a beating, malice, or deprivation. However, the husband should be more understanding as to why she is not in the mood for sex. He also should be willing to put in the work to get her in the mood for sex, thereby ensuring that both parties are adequately satisfied. Sex is not an act that was made to be enjoyed by one party; however, if the husband has the "handmaiden wife" mentality then he would not care if she is in the mood and does not try to get her in the mood as a "queen wife." Instead, he expects her to make herself available only to satisfy his need.

Thankfully, the mindset of a wife who is solely dependent on the husband financially is now changing and being challenged. Therefore, the ability of some husbands to use their money as a "power tool" for control is greatly diminished.

Story 8

A story is told of a couple who traveled around frequently. And when they did, the wife would travel with all the cooking equipment that she would need to cook for her husband. She would set up a makeshift kitchen in their hotel or in the house of their host to resume her cooking because her husband would not eat any other food outside the home. So while in the hotel or a host house, she had no rest from her cooking duties.

My Analysis:

Now let us assume the wife does not mind the constant cooking and believes she needs to tend to all of her husband's needs. However, if the husband has the mentality of his wife as a "queen wife," then he should be able to ask her to take a break from cooking once in a while, which I believe she would not mind from time to time, especially when they are traveling outside the home. This would allow them to eat out sometimes, especially if there was no health issues that would prevent him from eating outside the home. In this case, he did not have any health condition that prevented him from eating out.

Story 9

Another story is told of a couple in which the wife gets back from work at about 11 p.m., and the husband gets back at 6 p.m. However, the husband will not fix dinner for himself or his wife. He would rather chill and idly wait for the wife to get back home to make him dinner, even if it was late at night.

There is also another case in which the wife had to go to work while her husband was off work and was at home. But the husband would wait for his wife to return from work to prepare him a meal, even though he has been at home all day idling away the time.

Yet there was another case in which the wife would cook for her husband; however, unless she dished the food for her husband, he would not serve the meal for himself whenever he desired. He would expect the meal to be served to him. Because he is of the mindset that taking the food from the fridge or microwaving the food is too much work, and it is not a man's job.

My Analysis:

One can see the "handmaiden wife" mentality at play here. The first two husbands have the mentality that it is the wife's duty to make and serve their meal. So even if they could make their wives job easier by helping her with dinner before she gets back from work, they did not help because it not their duty, even though they knew how to fix up a meal.

I remember a time when my friends and I were much younger; we encountered a young man who could cook so well. We knew this because he had made a very delicious meal for us. My friends and I were extolling his virtues as a great cook, and we told him that his wife would be blessed to marry him because he could help her with the cooking. However, he immediately countered us, saying that he would never let his wife know he could cook or had ever cooked, so she would not take advantage of him and expect him to help her with the cooking! So even though he was a great cook, his wife would never enjoy that aspect of his life because he already assumed it was solely his wife's job to cook and he would not help her, so she does not get to take advantage of him. This is such an unhealthy mentality and assumption.

In the case of the third husband, I would like to clarify that it is not wrong if a wife dishes and serves her husband's meal. It is a noble thing, and it is encouraged. However, if the wife is not available or able to serve her husband for whatever reason, it should not be a big deal if the husband serves himself whenever he wants to eat, as this will not strip him of his manhood. Now, if a wife goes out of her way to cook the meal in the home but her husband refuses to serve himself because he is of the mindset that he is the man and his wife must dish and serve his food, then this is not a healthy mindset. It is that "handmaiden wife" mentality creeping up again, and this mentality promotes a lot of laziness and so much dependence on the woman. Because of this mindset, some husbands are unable to help themselves or take care of anything when their wives are not available or not at home. For example, some husbands usually have no idea where their socks or shoes are in the home or how to turn on the stove to make a simple meal or how to heat up a meal in the microwave or even make tea for themselves; instead, they are dependent on their wives and need help for almost everything.

Now I must admit that certain women to a large extent have fueled this mentality; they have often given the impression that they are "superwomen" or "saviors" who can fix everything, which fuels a culture of laziness in their husbands. Then they turn around and complain about being stressed out and not getting adequate or any help from their husbands. It is time that these women put off their "superwomen capes" and ask for help and also receive the help offered from their husbands.

Nowadays, if a wife is expected to work and earn money to help her husband increase the family's income—especially when the husband's income is not enough to meet all their expenses—then it should not be a crime or a sin if the wife expects her husband to help her around the house. If she helps him with the financial responsibility, then he should be able to help her with the chores in the home.

I believe reciprocity is what we should adopt with each other because God never intended for the wife or the husband to be selfish and receive all the help from their spouse without helping them in return, even nature shows us reciprocity in many areas. Looking around, we will see reciprocity even in the simple things. For example, in handwashing, the right hand washes the left hand and the left hand, in turn, washes the right hand. Taking an example from nature, an animal eats grass; this animal, in turn, excretes dung onto the grass; and this fertilizes the land, which helps the grass to grow. Plants release oxygen that animals and humans breathe in, and humans in turn breathe out carbon dioxide that plants use to survive. So plants and animals nourish themselves in nature's carbon cycle. The water that evaporates from the earth's surface into the atmosphere (removing heat), comes back down again as rain to water the earth's surface. The tree that extracts nutrients from the soil, in turn, sheds leaves that replenishes the soil. A lot more things around us in nature display reciprocity; they add to something, and the things they add to, in turn, nourishes them in return. This is God's replenishing system of life. Moreover, in instances where there is no reciprocity, one party diminishes or dies. Maybe God is trying to teach us something that is never to be comfortable, constantly getting from others and not giving back in return, especially in the marriage relationship. Let us look at the break down of the following three kinds of relationships[2] and compare them to marriage today:

1. **Commensal Relationship:** This describes a relationship between two living organisms in which one benefits and the other is not significantly harmed or helped. In regard to a marriage relationship, one party enjoys the benefit of the union while the other party does not benefit anything. A marriage should never be a commensal relationship. Sadly, however, a lot of marriage relationships are commensal. In this kind of relationship, there usually is a "free rider" or a "bum" who thrives. In this case, the "free riders" keep receiving all the love, attention, resources, and care; but they never give anything significant back to their spouses. So their spouses are not significantly harmed but are not helped either, so the marriage relationships add no real value to their spouses.

2. **Paralytic Relationship:** Marriage should not be a paralytic relationship either. In this kind of relationship; one party gains, and the other party is harmed. In regard to a marriage relationship, one enjoys all the benefits of the union, while the other party suffers. A narcissistic

---

2 These three relationships are adapted from the *Wikipedia* article "Symbiosis" found at <https://en.wikipedia.org/wiki/Symbiosis>.

person will usually thrive in this situation at the detriment of the other party. In this case, narcissistic spouses have an excessive need for admiration, disregard for their spouses' feelings, have an inability to handle any criticism, and have a sense of entitlement. Everything revolves around them. And they do not care if their partners suffer in the process, so their spouses are harmed emotionally and psychologically, as they suffer some form of neglect and abandonment from their spouses.

3. **Mutualistic Relationship:** As we have seen, the marriage relationship should not be commensal or paralytic; this is not God's intention. Instead, marriage should be more of a mutualistic relationship; this kind of relationship describes a long-term relationship between individuals of different species where both individuals benefit. And in relation to a marriage relationship, this kind of relationship describes a healthy, loving relationship in which the husband and wife meet each other's needs and are both nourished.

Story 10

I also heard a story in which the man's wife had left the house to attend to her personal business and needed to proceed from there to an important meeting; however, her husband—who was at home—required her to return home first and make him some food before she went back out to her meeting. So even though he was at home and not doing anything, he refused to warm or make a simple meal for himself but required his wife to go out of her way to return home and make his food before she could attend her meeting.

My Analysis:

This is still the same superiority mentality and "handmaiden wife" mindset on display because the husband needed to be served by the wife. Even though his wife was not home, she had to be called back home to perform her duties. This story is similar to story 3 in which the wife had to stop cooking to attend to the baby while her husband watched TV. This is deeply rooted in a lot of cultures, and some men even boast about how much "control" they have over their wives. By their standards, the more control the husbands have over their wives, the stronger and more manly they are. However, nothing is farther from the truth; they reduce the marriage relationship to a boss-servant relationship. God did not give the man the assignment of controlling his wife; instead, the assignment He gave was for the husband to love his wife. However, some husbands have unconsciously entered into competition with other husbands and, in turn, get so worked up about how they cannot control their wives; and they struggle endlessly to seek to control their wives. Even God does not control us, instead He allows us to make our choices.

Performing roles in the home does not make or break the husband's leadership. Leadership is a state of mind; and if you do not see yourself as a leader, suppressing others will not make you a leader. Instead, it will only give you a false sense of being a leader. A leader has influence; he does not make people do things to make him feel validated. People willingly follow and work with an effective leader without any coercion or manipulation from him.

Story 11
Domestic Violence:

There are several stories of women who have been beaten or still are being beaten by their husbands.

Some of them have even died in the process.

Some wives were beaten or abused for minor offenses such as:

1. not having the husband's food ready on time,

2. not tidying up the house as expected,

3. not attending to the kids as expected,

4. not doing all the other household chores as expected, and

5. not doing what they were asked to do.

Some wives were beaten or abused for major offenses such as:

6. talking back in an argument,

7. showing disrespect toward their husbands or others,

8. insulting their husbands,

9. spending money without the appropriate or expected permission,

10. not submitting their paycheck to their husbands,

11. leaving home or staying out late,

12. suspicion of cheating or actual cheating on their husbands by the wives, and

13. refusing to have sex with their husbands, and so forth.

The list of so-called punishable crimes are extensive and cannot be exhausted here.

My Analysis:

Sadly, most victims of domestic violence have been reprimanded by others sometimes, even by other women, that it is their fault their husbands beat them. And if they were submissive enough or had done what they were supposed to do, then their husbands would not have beaten them. This sort of reasoning is faulty.

Some of the victim-blaming women were also beaten and mistreated by their husbands, so they have accepted it as the norm and expect other women to suffer what they have suffered as well. I once heard of an older woman that was admonishing a younger wife who was being beaten by her husband at the time; the older woman told the young wife she needed to be "trained" by her husband. She stated when she was a younger wife, her husband also beat her. She told the young wife to allow her husband to continue to beat her and not complain or report him to anyone; thus, when she gets older, she will be wiser and better "trained." And then her grown kids will help stop the husband from beating her further.

Some other wives believe the lie that they ought to be beaten by their husbands for the sake of correction. And some others believe, when they are beaten, they are guaranteed to be given "gifts" for reconciliation.

I had heard of a woman who would sometimes say to herself, "Mrs. ——, you are not thinking right; oh, Mr. —— will need to beat you, so you can think right." This was a terrible mindset she had; she must have experienced and was made to believe that women ought to be beaten, so they can think and act right.

No woman is to be blamed for violence towards her by her husband. The victim is never to be blamed for the violent actions of a perpetrator towards them. As a society, we need to challenge and change that mentality of victim blaming.

If a man sees his wife like a queen who ought to be cherished and pampered, then he would treat her like one. A queen is respected, doors opened for her, chairs pulled out for her to sit on, and she is well taken care of. She is not a handmaiden or servant for her husband to use as a "punching bag" in order to channel his anger. Uncontrolled anger is also a major reason why a man would hit his wife.

I would encourage any man reading this book, who is dealing with anger problems, to seek God's face. Meditate on God's Word that deals with anger. Seek anger management classes, seek accountability partners, seek counseling, and seek as many options as possible to help with your anger. Your wife is not your problem, but the devil is; this is confirmed in Ephesians 6:12, which says, "For we are not fighting against human beings but against the wicked spiritual forces in the heavenly world, the rulers, authorities, and cosmic powers of this dark age" (GNT). Therefore, channel your anger to the right recipient and fight him in the place of prayer and knowledge. Your wife was not given to you to be the subject of your anger. Like Pastor Creflo Dollar would always say, "A man that can't control his anger emotions but is instead governed and ruled by his emotions is the weakest man on earth." If anger has power to control your actions and determines how you would react in any given situation or make you act beyond control, then anger is more powerful than you are. And you have no control over it, instead it has control over you. It is okay to be angry, but it is not okay to stay angry or use that as an excuse to hit your spouse. Please seek help before the devil destroys you and your family.

My mentor Bishop T. D. Jakes once said that in all his years of counseling married couples, he has never seen a man who raised his hands against his wife that loved or felt good about himself. This shows that hitting one's spouse is a direct correlation of self-hate projected onto someone else and sometimes manifested through anger.

Slave masters used to beat and mistreat their slaves into submission as they pleased because the slaves belonged to them; however, this is not the case in a marriage relationship. You do not own your spouse, and she is not your slave. She is royalty and should be treated as such.

Story 12

Breadwinner:

There are so many stories of wives being the breadwinner in the home, while their husbands barely worked or did not even work at all. I will not be able to recount all the individual encounters but will lump them all together as one. Some of the women in these cases worked so hard to make ends meet; but they had little or no help from their husbands, who were the ones who were ideally supposed to meet the family finances. Some husbands even demand for their wives to hand over their paychecks to them, which they disbursed as they wished. Sometimes, they even disbursed the funds selfishly or extravagantly without any consideration to their wives or their wives' input.

My Analysis:

Let us remember what the Bible says in 1 Timothy 5:8, "People who don't take care of their relatives, and especially their own families, have given up their faith. They are worse than someone who doesn't have faith in the Lord" (CEV). I believe this is the only biblical reference where a believer is regarded as being worse than an unbeliever, so it must be a very serious issue. Now if the Bible says that a man who puts his hand on the plow and looks back is not fit for the kingdom of God (Luke 9:62) and then the Bible compares a person who refuses to provide for his family as one who has lost the faith (1 Timothy 5:8), that then goes to shows how much God frowns upon not providing for one's own family.

Now I am not referring to a husband who lost his job or business and is working hard to get back on his feet. In this case, I believe the wife should do all she can to help lift up her husband and get him back on his feet financially. However, it becomes a problem when a man falls to his feet financially and refuses to get back up and has so many excuses for not meeting up with his responsibilities. And he is perfectly fine with his wife taking care of the financial responsibilities of the family while he barely does anything or sits around the house.

Now I believe a man who is not working at all and a man who is working at less than his capacity both fall into the same category. For example, if a husband has the ability to work at 100% capacity but works at only 10% capacity, he is in the same category as the husband who is not working and providing for his family. He cannot talk about meeting his financial responsibilities, especially when his family is falling behind financially.

In some cases, wives who were supposed to be the helpers have become the burden bearers; but they were never made to bear the whole financial burden. And even though the woman is bearing the responsibility of the home in most of these stories, she also is still expected to fulfill her traditional role in the house with little or no help from the husband. Since God decided that it was not good for the man to be alone and brought a woman into the man's life to help him, then it is not right for a woman to bear all the family's burden without any help from her husband.

Let us imagine a scenario in which a man (husband) has the task of fulfilling his destiny, building a family and meeting the family's responsibilities; and so he marries a helper (wife) who can strengthen and help him, and she assists him in fulfilling his destiny and to also bear the family responsibilities in order to prevent him from being overwhelmed. Now let us imagine another situation where the husband's tasks of building a family and meeting the family responsibilities are now fully transferred to the helper (wife) while the one being helped (husband) assumes little or no responsibility. If the Bible makes reference to the wife as the weaker vessel, then she should not be made to bear all of the family's responsibilities.

In Genesis 2:15: "The Lord God placed the man in the Garden of Eden to tend and watch over it" (NLT). In this Bible verse, we can see that God gave the man (Adam) work before he brought the woman (Eve) onto the scene. A husband needs to get his "work" together before bringing in a woman into his life, and even if his "work" temporarily gets lost along the way after they are married; this is fine, provided that the husband does not make this a permanent situation and works hard to restore what was lost.

I can guarantee that husbands will not get the best from wives who are solely bearing all the financial responsibilities. They are not supposed to carry such burdens. That is why you see some wives in those situations get easily aggressive, irritable, frustrated, or stressed out. Because the financial security these women expect and crave from their husbands is lacking, and now they need to provide that security for themselves and their families. In some cases, you see the wife easily "snap" at her husband at the slightest provocation.

Even if the wife has a good job that can sustain the family and is fine with being the breadwinner, I still believe the husband should be working on something because it is about fulfilling a purpose and building a legacy; and a man cannot be achieving any of these by doing nothing.

If you are a husband reading this book and you are not meeting your financial responsibilities, or you are working less than your capacity—notwithstanding if it is your fault or not—please do not be comfortable taking a back seat financially, no matter how long it has been. Instead, pray and ask God for His help, get out of your comfort zone, and make things happen—nothing is going to fall into your lap. If you have faith, add works to your faith, get out there into the world, and take what belongs to you. If you cannot get a job because no one will hire you, then create a job or start a business or provide a service or go back to school. However, do not believe and accept the lie of the enemy that there nothing more you can do, no matter how old you are; your wife, children, grandchildren, and legacy are still counting on you. Do not count yourself out!

Story 13
Cheating:

There are many sad stories of husbands who have cheated or are still cheating on their wives with other women, with little or no remorse for their actions (and sadly, even wives cheating on their husbands as well). In some of these cases, the husbands have completely abandoned their wives and children for other women, sometimes even leaving their spouses for family members or for friends. Also, in some of these cases, the cheating spouse has brought a sexually transmitted disease into the union that eventually killed both spouses and left their children orphaned. There are so many of such stories that I cannot individually describe.

My Analysis:

In general, some men have the mentality that it is in men's nature to cheat (which they blame on their testosterone). They expect their wives to not be surprised or feel betrayed by their actions and expect their wives to get over their indiscretions. However, husbands with this mentality cannot imagine getting over being cheated on by their wives. How do they expect their wives to accept such immorality if they cannot even imagine their wives cheating on them?

Some women even get blamed for the reasons their husbands cheated on them. Some of the reasons include:

1. The wife does not give the husband good sex and is unable to "perform" in bed.

2. The wife does not take care of herself and is no longer attractive.

3. She does not cook good food that appeals to her husband.

4. She is lazy.

5. She has had children and is no longer sexually attractive.

6. She is not giving her husband enough attention.

7. She nags and is not respectful enough.

8. She does not pray enough.

9. She is not submissive enough.

10. She has gained a lot of weight and has become sloppy.

There are so many other unbelievable reasons. However, in all these reasons, the responsibility of the man to control his lust is mostly thrown away because it is almost solely the wife's responsibility to reign in her husband. Moreover, when she is unable to reign him in, she is seen as the one who has failed maritally. This expectation sets a woman on an absurd, perpetual cycle of working to ensure she reigns in her husband; and most times, this leaves the man with barely any responsibility to tame his own desires. Therefore, if the wife falls short, and the husband cheats, the wife then gets the blame.

A wife (queen) ought to be precious and thus treated as such. Her heart should not be a tool to play games with or to test how cool or "manly" the husband think he still is. She is made in the image of God and should be cherished and treated as such. A woman was not made to be an instrument for a man's pleasure; she is a speaking spirit and has the life of God in her. She should not be cheated on or with for whatever reason.

10 Roles Do Not Negate Leadership

When the term role is referenced here, it is in relation to the household duties or chores. Some men are of the mindset that if they engage in the chores around the house then they are robbed of their manhood. However, this is so far from the truth. Helping around the house does not diminish men in any way; instead, it adds to their character.

Imagine a husband avoiding household chores because he is of the mind-set that he is the "man" and the "boss" in the house; and as such, he cannot lower himself to taking on any household assignment that he feels is his wife's responsibility. Now this is a husband who does not understand that he is still the head of the household because God said he is the head—whether or not he works alongside his wife; it does not rob him of his leadership. Sadly, however, most people see leaders, not as those who serve, but as the "bosses" that need to be served and attended to by the ones they lead.

Let us analyze the example of Jesus in John 13 4–5: "so he got up from the meal, took off his outer clothing, and wrapped a towel around his waist. After that, he poured water into a basin and began to wash his disciples' feet, drying them with the towel that was wrapped around him" (NIV).

In the Bible passage referenced above, even though Jesus is the Savior of the world, He was still able to stoop low and wash the feet of the disciples. It was a symbolic act that He undertook; therefore, we can see that even as leaders, we ought to serve others. Washing the feet of the disciples did not take away from Jesus' leadership; instead, it added to His stature. The people of the world wait for others to serve them, but Kingdom people should be willing to be of service to others, even as leaders.

In a marriage relationship, the husband and wife should be team players; and when they become team players, then they can both work together as a team and achieve a lot more together. And, consequently, when any member of the "couple" team is available and able and there is a task to be completed, that member of the team does not ignore the task because of the faulty mindset that the task is the other party's responsibility and in the process becomes a shirker. Instead, they cover each other's back and help the "marriage" team succeed.

Chapter Four

Is Your Wife Your Queen or Your Handmaiden?

∼❧∼

11 Do Some or All These Points Apply to You?

Now let us critically assess our mindset as it relates to some of the case studies we just examined and assess which mindset is ours.

Do some or all of these points apply to a husband? Here are telltale signs that reveal a husband who does not regard his wife as his queen:

1. He does not honor her and speaks disrespectfully to her in private and in public, even without any provocation.

2. He rarely communicates with her; and the times he does, it is solely to pass out instructions of what he wants her to do for him or for the children.

3. When she is sick or incapacitated, he is upset about the burden of having to take care of her and having to do all the household chores. He even gets irritated that she is taking too long to recover.

4. He cannot hold her hand and be affectionate with her in public, or he is ashamed to be seen with her in public.

5. He keeps receiving from her but rarely give anything back in return. Is her duty primarily to meet the husband's needs only, while hers are neglected? This is dysfunctional. God expects reciprocity (to receive and to give) in human relationships; that is why God did not make any of us self-sufficient or independent. There are so many examples around us; even God's creatures and creation teach us that it is not acceptable to be "receivers" and not "givers." Why then is there the

mindset that such a behavior would be acceptable in a marriage relationship?

6. She is not worthy of his time and commitment. Spending time with her feels like a waste of time to him. He feels like he is missing out on more "important" things such as his TV shows, work, sports, hanging out with his friends, and so forth. He could spend hours binge-watching several cable shows or hanging out with his friends; but personal time spent with his wife irritates and angers him because he perceives it as a waste of his precious time.

7. No matter how hard she works, it is never good enough. He keeps making demands of her but never appreciate what she has already done for him.

8. When she speaks in public, he is embarrassed of her and wants her to keep quiet, or he shuts her up.

9. Can he take on any household task while his wife relaxes? Or would it upset him that she needs to be doing something while he is doing a household task? Is she entitled to any time to relax? Does he regard that it as an abomination that he is performing a chore and his wife has the nerve to take a break?

   I once heard a man proclaim it would be an abomination for his wife to be watching TV while he cooks; and that he would never subscribe to the "American idea" that they should take turns doing the household chores. However, I longed to ask him: would it an abomination if it was the other way around or would that be normal and accepted? As most of the time that is the scenario in many households. The wife is doing a lot of chores in the home, while the husband is relaxed watching television and sometimes making more demands of her as well.

10. Does he ridicule or make fun of her, or make her the butt of his jokes with others and thus make her a laughing stock?

11. His wife and children are afraid of him; that is, his presence elicits terror, and everyone scrambles when he is around. He is virtually a "terrorist" in his own home.

12. Does he see his wife as an intelligent person with whom he can discuss politics, career, and business and not as a handmaiden that he

cannot relate to? Or is his discussion with her solely to pass information about the kids and nothing more? Only pride would make a husband think he is the only smart one, while he regards his wife as an unintelligent person whom he cannot talk or interact with. If he was the smartest one, then he would not have ended up marrying a wife with a "low IQ."

12 A King's Mentality as He Relates to His Queen

Do some or all of these apply to you? Here are some telltale signs that reveal if a man regards his wife as his queen:

1. He makes a constant effort to communicate and interact with his wife regularly.

2. He regards, appreciates, and honors his wife. He does not speak to her disrespectfully and will not let anyone do the same.

3. He is chivalrous and not condescending towards her; for example, he opens the door for her, pulls out the chair for her, holds her hand when walking with her, and so forth.

4. He does not look down on his wife or criticize and condemn her, while he sees himself as the superior being.

5. He is patient with her, just as he expects her to be patient with him.

6. He is not intimidated by her success or by her being a powerful woman. He does not try to compete with her, put her down, or try to end her success so he can be elevated; instead, he cheers and encourages her to succeed.

7. He does not mistreat or lay his hands on her because she is valued and held in high esteem.

8. He helps her with the household chores, and he does not sit idly by and allows his wife to work until she becomes stressed out. He does not have to be nagged, coerced, or forced to help her.

9. He does not see her as a slave whose whole existence is to serve him and fulfill all his needs but without any needs of her own. He is thankful when she does things for him.

10. He goes out of his way to make her happy and satisfied.

11. He does not make a mockery of her.

13 Practical Steps to Take When You Are Treated or Regarded as a Handmaiden Wife

1. **Pray:** Talk to God about how you feel and how you are being treated. Ask Him to teach you what to do. He is able to give you the best strategy for your unique situation.

2. **Forgive your spouse:** Endeavor to forgive your spouse for every hurtful way he has knowingly or unknowingly treated you. You cannot shine as the royalty God has made you to be if you hang on to resentment and bitterness towards your spouse. Forgiving your spouse helps you more than it helps your spouse. Like my mentor always says, it is not the storm that beats against a boat that sinks it, but it is what gets into it that sinks it. Forgive your spouse so you do not sink your "boat." Your royal heart was not built to harbor the chaff of unforgiveness, it would crash under its weight.

3. **Share how you feel with your spouse:** Let your husband know what your expectations are and how you will like him to help out. Do not expect your husband to instantly understand your feelings or to instantly change. Do not be tempted to nag and complain. You might have to talk about how you feel several times, but you should do this in a loving and calm way.

4. **Be tactfully patient:** An ingrained mindset does not change overnight; it takes awhile—sometimes a really long time. Your husband may be working with an archaic mindset that he saw his parents use, and he might stubbornly refuse to be open to a better mindset. Sometimes this may be due to the fear that his "place" will be taken. You can help allay such fears by explaining that treating you

as a queen and helping you does not change him from being a king; instead, it solidifies his position as a king and not a manservant. People generally do not like change. They might fight you very hard at first; but with time, teachings and encouragement, ingrained mindsets can gradually change.

Moreover, if your spouse's mindset never changes, be content with being the royalty God said you are, and shine like one. Do not let the way your spouse treats you affect how you see yourself.

5. **Increase your knowledge:** Attend marriage seminars in which you can both be further enlightened, and then any wrong mindset can be addressed and corrected.

6. **Be courteous:** Respectfully show your spouse how you want to be treated.

7. **Share things together:** Get involved in your spouse's recreational activities and hobbies so you both can have something you can share together, so you do not drift apart.

8. **Solicit assistance:** Ask your spouse and others for help. Do not try to be a super woman in public and then silently die in secret or be bitter, murmur, and nag.

9. **Be fiscally accountable:** Do not take on more financial burden than you can bear. Do not worry about keeping up with the Joneses; you will be better off for it.

10. **Share responsibilities:** Involve the kids and others in the household responsibilities as much as you can.

11. **Consider paid services:** Hire paid help if you are financially able, so as to alleviate the responsibilities that are beyond your control (e.g., maid service, nanny, and so forth).

12. **Take your responsibilities in stride:** It is fine even if you are not able to get help. Do not become stressed out about doing all the household chores at a specific time, even when you are worn out and need to rest. Do your best every time you can. Remember the earth will not stop spinning because there are dirty dishes or laundry to be done. The kids and everyone would be fine if you take a little time

off to rest and rejuvenate. If you are gone, they will still survive. So do not send yourself to an early grave because you have to take care of everyone else but forget to take care of yourself. Your family needs the healthy, happy, rejuvenated "you" and not the tired, grumpy, nagging, and stressed out "you."

This is so important because I have heard of many stories about women who have worked themselves to death. Sometimes they worked several jobs to meet their financial responsibilities while also working to meet the responsibilities on the home front. These women did not pay attention to themselves until they slumped or ended up in the hospital. Do not add to the statistics!

Chapter Five

As a Wife or Husband, How Do You See Yourself?

How a woman perceives and views herself is very important. Now it is one thing to say a husband needs to treat his wife as his queen, but all that will be futile if the wife does not see herself as one. No matter what her husband does to treat her like a queen, she would still see herself as a handmaiden. Like I always tell my kids, "if you believe 'it,' then you become 'it' (whatever 'it' is)."

Sometimes over the course of a woman's life, she may have been looked down on, treated like a second-class citizen by people around her, and sometimes despised by her parents. Sadly, she may have even been molested. All of these events may have had negative consequences on how she perceives herself, such that she sees herself as less than she ought to. Therefore, she goes into marriage with that low-class mentality; and even if her husband treats her as a handmaiden, she is okay with it because she already sees herself as one.

Moreover, a man cannot see his wife like a queen if he does not see himself as a king. If he has a low self-esteem of himself, then he actually cannot see someone else in better esteem. Also, if he does not love himself, he cannot love or cherish another person.

As a man or a woman, you need to realize that you are created in the image and likeness of God (Genesis 1:26). God declares in His Word that we are kings and priests and shall reign on the earth. Revelation 5:10 says, Christ has "made us kings and priests to our God; and we shall reign on the earth" (NKJV). It is so important that we renew our minds and start seeing ourselves the way God sees us; if not, we cannot attain the destiny

God has ordained for our marriages and even beyond our marriages. This is so important because we see how the children of Israel perceived themselves as stated in the Bible, and ended up missing their destiny

"Everyone we saw was very tall, and we even saw giants there, the descendants of Anak. We felt as small as grasshoppers, and that is how we must have looked to them" (Number 13:32–33, GNT).

In another translation: "All the people we saw were huge. We even saw giants there, the descendants of Anak. Next to them we felt like grasshoppers, and that's what they thought, too!" (Number 13:32–33, NLT).

They called themselves "grasshoppers" even before the enemy thought or saw them as such creatures. And because they declared they were "grasshoppers," their enemy perceived them as such. The 400 years of slavery, could have affected how they perceived themselves and made them see themselves as less than or inferior to their enemies, but God did all the great miracles in the wilderness so they could reimagine and renew their minds and begin to see themselves as God saw them. He went to great lengths to save them because they belonged to Him, and they were a great people with the backing of a great God. However, they chose to keep seeing themselves as they used to be: mere slaves. Thus, they could not enter the promised land except for just two people: Joshua and Caleb.

You might be a husband or wife reading this book with a bad experience that has scarred you and left you looking down on yourself. However, I would like to remind you that you are a king and a queen, so step out in confidence into what God has said you are and enjoy being treated like royalty—and treating your spouse as royalty, too.

14 How to See Yourself as Royalty

1. **Believe in yourself and see yourself as God sees you:** God is royalty, and so He created and sees His children as such. Do not believe the lie of the devil that you are no good—just existing on the earth and marking time. If God declares you are royalty, then that is what you

are. Renewing your mind and exposing yourself to God's Word will help you see yourself as God sees you and cancel out the effects of the negative situation that you might have experienced in life. Carry and treat yourself like royalty.

2. **Celebrate and take care of yourself:** When you see yourself as royalty, you begin to take care and value yourself as one. In turn, this will reflect on your attitude and disposition in life. Thus, you will begin to reflect who and what you are, and it will be easy for people to treat you like the royalty you are because you see yourself as one.

3. **Empower yourself:** Be the best version of yourself that you can ever be, whatever that means to you. For some it might mean going back to school, or if possible, to learn a trade, to read books, to seek information, to exercise, and so forth. Do not allow yourself to be at the mercy of others financially, physically, and emotionally.

4. **Have a positive disposition about life:** Be happy and like yourself. Nobody wants to be around a grouch; being a grouch is an automatic "repellent." Life can sometimes throw so much at you that it is hard to hold your head up and be happy all the time; but you need to learn to find your core—that is, who you are at your core, what are your core values, what matters most to you, and look for reasons to be happy. That way your happiness comes from within and not from what is happening around you.

5. **Know who you are:** You cannot know who you are except when you go back to the One who made you and read His manual (God's Word), which tells you who you are. He says a lot in his Word about who we are: "You are gods" (Psalm 82:6, GNT), "You are like salt for the whole human race" (Matthew 5:13–16, GNT), you are loved (John 3:16), "For in Christ Jesus you are all sons of God, through faith" (Galatians 3:26, esv), and so forth. There is so much revealed truth in the Bible that would help anyone suffering from identity issues to know and understand who he or she is.

There is a story told of a bird whose egg became mixed with the eggs of some ducklings, and the mother duckling sat and hatched all the eggs together. However, when the eggs hatched one of them did not look like the others. Every time, the other ducklings would make fun of the odd bird because he did not look like them. One day, however, he caught his reflection in the water and noticed he did not look like the ducklings around him; he looked like the bird he had seen flying high in the sky. Upon discovery of his true identity he join his fellow bird and flew up in the sky like the majestic swan he had always been.

Like my chancellor (Bishop David Oyedepo) at Covenant University in Ota, Nigeria, always used to say, "There is no mountain anywhere; every man's mountain is his ignorance." If you do not know you are royalty, then you will settle for less. That is why a book like this one among many others seeks to show and remind you who you are. Do not see yourself any less.

15 Our Responsibilities

Husband's Responsibility

Even if you think your wife is not a queen and does not deserve to be treated like one, a key assignment for you as a king is to see and treat your wife as the queen she is—whether she is purely a potential queen or has matured into one in reality. Often, queens are not coronated when you meet them, nor are kings crowned when you encounter them (Bishop T. D. Jakes). Thus, your lifelong duty as a couple is to continuously bring out the queen or king in your spouse by the way you treat them, and it starts first with the right mindset. You can work to create what you have envisioned in your mind.

Wife's Responsibility

See yourself as a queen married to a king, whether the king is already crowned (perceives himself to be one and acts like one) or yet to be crowned (does not perceive himself as one nor acts like one) because sometimes people treat you the way you see yourself. The Israelites thought they were like grasshoppers, so they were in their own eyes and also in the eyes of their enemy. Though this book seeks to admonish a husband to treat his wife like a queen, but if the wife continually refuses to see and act like the queen she is, it would be likened to casting pearls before swine (Matthew 7:6) because the swine would never acknowledge or appreciate what is put in front of them. Refuse to think of yourself as a lowly servant who is fortunate that your husband married you; instead, think of yourself as a valuable person to whom your husband is blessed and fortunate to be married to. Like my mentor would frequently say, "How you allow people to treat you is a reflection of how you see yourself."

Treat your husband like the king that he is, as well; it should not be a one-way street. Even though the central theme of this book has been on the husband elevating and treating his wife as royalty, that does not mean the wife should expect that she should only be treated like royalty and not treat her husband as royalty in return (that is part of the reciprocity we have previously discussed).

Personal Responsibility

You do not have to wait for someone to see you as the royalty that you are, even if your spouse never gets to acknowledge or treat you like royalty. Do not let that become your problem; instead, see and treat yourself as royalty. Do not let yourself become angry or resentful about how anyone treats you because ultimately how you see and treat yourself is much more important. Do your best at all times, celebrate yourself, love yourself, and be happy. Do not let your happiness or self-love be dependent on how another person treats you because, if you do not love yourself, you cannot extend any love to others. You were fearfully and wonderfully made (Psalm 139:14), so carry yourself as such.

And, even if you are unmarried, divorced, or a single mother or father, do not wait for someone else to give you your validation or to make you feel like royalty. You are royalty because God said so. I want to remind you of that in this book; so square your shoulders, raise your head high (not in pride, though), and enjoy your life like the queen or king you ought to be.

Chapter Six

Change Your Mindset, Improve Your Marriage

I believe a husband should be regarded and treated like a king who is married to a queen; but if he is matched with a handmaiden, then that is a mismatch. A king is usually married to a queen, not a handmaiden. So a king should not treat or act like his wife is beneath him or is a handmaiden because, if he does, then he goes from being a king to becoming a manservant. This is because a manservant is paired with a handmaiden, and they fit together.

A king cannot lay his hands on a queen. It is a husband with a wrong mentality that would think it is his duty to correct his wife by hitting or mishandling her in any way. Instead, he needs the correction he is trying to give out. It is a parent's duty to train their children; but if a husband thinks it is his duty to help his wife's parent complete or continue with her "training," then that husband is no king but a manservant. It is not the husband's duty to beat or coerce his wife into submission. Rather, being a responsible, God-fearing leader and showing her love will automatically make the wife respond with submission and respect. It is only a man with an inferiority mindset who would think his wife is less than he is or is not properly "trained" and needs to be corrected by beating his wife.

In the past I have heard some bachelors suggest that they cannot wait to get married, so their wife's can start taking care of them and so they can stop doing all the household chores they are currently doing. However, they are often only thinking of themselves. A woman should not come into marriage solely to perform all the responsibilities the man is tired of taking care of; instead, she should come into her husband's life to help and complement what he is already doing. Sometimes, these men see marriage solely as acquiring a free lifetime handmaiden with whom they can also have sex with.

Some men have gotten married based on the sole criteria that they are looking for a wife who is a "domesticated" woman and not a "destinated" (i.e., a destiny-minded) woman; they end up missing the main point. It is not necessarily a bad thing to seek a domesticated woman since no one wants a lazy wife; however, that should not be the primary criteria. I strongly believe that in addition to looking for God's will in a prospective partner, one should look for a woman who is "whole" (spiritually, emotionally, physically, and so forth) and emotionally mature—not an emotional "terrorist" or a "drama queen" who would readily throw a tantrum or seek to control or manipulate everything and everyone around her in order to get her way. She should be someone who has a sense of purpose and intends to help her husband achieve his purpose in life, while achieving hers as well. This means the man should already know or seek to know what his purpose in life is; that way, he will seek a woman who can help him pursue and achieve his purpose, and he will appreciate her help.

Consciously or unconsciously, a lot of husbands—especially men from the continent of Africa—have the mentality that their spouses are their handmaidens. And even when these men have the ability to pick up after themselves or help with the dishes or warm up a meal or help with the kids, they would rather wait for their wives to do it for them or do it grudgingly (when coerced or nagged). Being married is not an automatic access to a personal maid who is disguised as a wife. Women have been made to believe that the wife's sole responsibility in life is to care and cater for her husband's and children's needs. They are not expected to have any needs; and even when they have, they are mostly unmet.

Now let us analyze this further: If you had a hired servant (that is, a housemaid or housegirl or houseboy, as they are popularly known in Africa), you would not start doing the hired servant's duties. Most masters who hire servants will not start feeling sorry for the hired servants because of all the duties the hired servants have to do. Moreover, they would not offer to help the hired servants perform their assignments because the masters have the mindset that the servants are being paid or contracted to do those duties. The hired servants would be expected to perform all the duties that they have been paid or contracted to do, and even more.

However, in a marriage relationship, the wife is not a hired servant. She is a companion, a queen, a helpmate. She ought to come alongside her husband to help him fulfill his God-given agenda. However, when she is seen as a handmaiden whose sole duties are (1) to give birth to children, (2) to take care of the children and her husband, (3) to do all the household chores, and (4) to work outside the home and mostly not expect to receive anything in return, then the mentality of a "handmaiden wife" becomes even more evident. As such, no one often feels sorry for her or offers to help her complete all the tasks that she has to do because she is regarded as the paid servant—like in the example in the paragraph above (only without pay in this case); she is expected to carry out all her responsibilities by herself. In some cases, you may see the wife spending hours cooking in the kitchen, cleaning around the house, and doing many other tasks while her husband and children sit around watching television, playing video games, or just being idle; her husband and kids most times do not feel a need to help her. Even when they do not help her, they do not feel guilty about it.

Husbands, please start reprogramming your mind! Your wife was never meant to be a "handmaiden wife," waiting on your every command while she is neglected. She is supposed to be a "queen wife" and also to be cherished. A husband working alongside his wife to meet the demands and responsibilities of the marriage and home and engaging with her leads to a happy, less stressed, and peaceful wife; which, in turn, leads to a happy home. Actively engaging with your wife tells her that you care for her; thus, it will make her want to go out of her way to make you happy; otherwise, you will both become "cellmates" in the same "prison."

I believe one of the goals of marriage should always be how to relieve each other's burden—not to add to the burden. We should be an asset to our spouses and not a liability. Your presence in your spouse's life should be an encouragement for his or her advancement, not a weight that pulls and drags him or her down. No one wants a liability but an asset. When we did not know better, we could not do better; but now we know better, then we must do better.

A lot of women are becoming stressed out by having to meet all the burdens and responsibilities of family life all by themselves. Some of them get bitter in the process.

Research has shown that prolonged stress can weaken a person's immune system, leaving them prone to various diseases. It can also increase the risk of digestive problems and depression. Chronic stress also can lead to the growth and spread of cancer in a number of ways.[3]

A husband should not be comfortable with the mentality that allows his wife to get all worked up and stressed out while he sits idly by because he thinks he is the master who needs to be served by his "handmaiden wife." This mentality needs to be addressed in our marriages, and it should not be regarded as alright or as a proper way of living. The mentality of the wife "slaving" continuously needs to be challenged; and many husbands have used the Bible verse in Ephesians 5:23, claiming that since husbands are the head of their wives then they have the right to boss or lord it over their wives.

If a husband wants to enjoy his wife and preserve her youthfulness, then he needs to help her in the home. He should not leave her all stressed out and exhausted because he will end up creating a nag, a "monster," and an unpleasant and unfriendly person out of his wife. Sadly though, when this happens, instead of fixing the problem, some husbands resort to going outside of their marriages to find friendly, pleasant companions to hang out with. They forget, however, that their wives used to be a

---

3 For more information on this issue visit <https://www.mdanderson.org/publications/focused-on-health/december-2014/how-stress-affects-cancer-risk.html>.

pleasant companions whom they always wanted to hangout with; that is why they decided to marry them in the first place. So what has changed?

Some men would complain that their wives are no longer pleasant to be around and they constantly nag about a lot of things. They compare their wives to their colleagues, friends, and others who are always nice and pleasant to them, with whom they want to hang out with. However, they fail to ask themselves a question, whether those pleasant companions will still be constantly pleasant and nice if they had to deal with the daily stressful situation and routine their wives have to go through. These men also fail to realize that constantly stressed out wives cannot just suck it up and be pleasant and nice all the time and not nag or act out their stress or frustration sometimes—that would be expecting too much from their wives. In addition, some husbands—instead of working to reduce or eliminate their wives' stress—expect their wives to still maintain the same level of stress and also maintain a constant pleasant attitude and not nag at them at the same time. First, husbands need to develop a sympathetic appreciation for what their wives go through, then that way they can put themselves in their wives' place and better be able to understand how their wives feel and be more willing to help them.

Some husbands have used submission as a license to treat their wives as slaves; to mistreat them; to use them for their selfish means; to demean and disrespect them; and to verbally, physically, and sexually abuse them. And any wife who questions this treatment is seen as rebellious and not submissive. How then do we explain these actions in light of the biblical injunction that a husband should love his wife. In fact, in the open heaven devotional of September 21, 2018, Pastor E. A. Adeboye speaks clearly about this mentality of a boss-servant marriage:

Theme: Not Your Subordinate[4]

> And the LORD God said, It is not good that the man should be alone; I will make him an help meet for him (Genesis 2:18).

---

4 This is cited from the *Open Heaven Daily Devotional* by Pastor E. A. Adeboye, Friday's devotion for September 21, 2018.

Likewise, ye husbands, dwell with them according to knowledge, giving honour unto the wife, as unto the weaker vessel, and as being heirs together of the grace of life; that your prayers be not hindered. Finally, be ye all of one mind, having compassion one of another, love as brethren, be pitiful, be courteous: Not rendering evil for evil, or railing for railing: but contrariwise blessing; knowing that ye are thereunto called, that ye should inherit a blessing (1 Peter 3:7–9).

Message:

The way some men relate with their wives is unbecoming of a child of God. Some husbands deal with their wives like a high handed boss would deal with an employee. When one beholds such sights, one begins to wonder whether it was love that brought them together in the first place or something else. They talk to their wives as if their wives are nonentities. Husbands who behave in this manner do not understand the essence of a woman in a man's life Genesis 2:18 says it all: "And the LORD God said, It is not good that the man should be alone; I will make him an help meet for him." What led to this divine decision, seen in Genesis 2:20, is equally intriguing: "And Adam gave names to all cattle, and to the fowl of the air, and to every beast of the field; but for Adam there was not found an help meet for him." We need to note some points from these two scriptures first of which is that as fearfully and wonderfully made as Adam was, he needed a helpmate, of which none was found amongst other creatures. God then decided to create a woman customized and tailored to meet this need. Secondly, men do not seek help from an inferior entity; at best, they look in the direction of an associate that is at least equal to their status. Thirdly, if Adam needed help, he required a quality helper to render it, and this was exactly what God provided. Therefore, any man who treats his wife as an inferior being cannot appreciate God's gift in the woman God has given him. This is an unfortunate situation. The word "weaker" used when describing women as vessels should not be taken to mean "inferior vessel"; rather, it is best interpreted as flexible vessels. Indeed, women are flexible, and they must be if they would serve the purpose for which they were created as helpmates of men. It is however, unfortunate that some men take advantage of the flexible nature of women to extort and manipulate them. The consequence of this terrible act is seen in Malachi 2:14: "Yet ye say,

Wherefore? Because the LORD hath been witness between thee and the wife of thy youth, against whom thou hast dealt treacherously: yet is she thy companion, and the wife of thy covenant." Furthermore, note that God is angry with domestic treachery and unfaithfulness. It has negative effects on your spirit and on the children of your union."

Conclusion

The purpose of this book is to enlighten the minds of husbands (kings) to understand and see their wives (queens) differently, and for wives to see themselves as they are in Christ. A wife is meant to be a helper and not to carry all the burden of overseeing and taking care of every aspect of the family's responsibilities; they should be shared responsibilities. How individual families share that responsibility is up to them personally; I am not advocating for a 50/50 role sharing. However, if the husband is able and available to help but refuses to lift a finger because he believes it is his wife's responsibility, then there is a problem with that mindset. Some husbands have a mindset that when they become more involved and help their wives (queens), then they will be taken advantage of; however, this is a wrong mindset and should not be the case because real team players do not take advantage of each other, instead they help each other succeed, that is what makes them a team.

This situation also applies to the wife who has the capacity and ability to help her husband with their finances, but she refuses to help him because she believes it is her husband's sole responsibility. Even if the man has to work multiple jobs to make ends meet, while the wife stays at home and spends or even wastes their limited resources; she does not care. This is not teamwork; instead, it is one party taking advantage of the other party. However, it is not wrong if the husband has a well-paying job (and does not have to work multiple jobs to meet their expenses) and his wife chooses to be a housewife who takes care of the home front and they are both fine with the arrangement.

The mindset of team members should be teamwork in which both husband and wife work together to build a great life. However, if one member bears most of the burden and the other party does not or barely lifts a finger to help, then this is no longer teamwork but a master-servant relationship and it is servitude, which is not God's original plan. God's initial plan was not for us to rule over or dominate each other, but for us to have dominion over the works of His hands as is evident in Genesis 1:28: "And God blessed them [granting them certain authority] and said to them, 'Be fruitful, multiply, and fill the earth, and subjugate it [putting it under your power]; and rule over (dominate) the fish of the sea, the birds of the air, and every living thing that moves upon the earth'" (AMP). However, as a result of the fall, ruling over the woman became the consequences as seen in Genesis 3:16: "… Yet your desire and longing will be for your husband, and he will rule [with authority] over you and be responsible for you" (AMP). However, Jesus came to bring us back to God's initial plan, which is for us to dominate over the things He created—not over each other. So the husband being the head of the home does not translate to being in a boss-servant relationship with his wife, because Christ's relationship with the Church is not a boss-servant relationship; thus, the husband's headship with his wife is supposed to be patterned after Christ and the Church.

My purpose with this book is to show how a lifelong mentality has plunged women into continuous servitude; and any woman who does not fit into the expected role is seen as an outcast and rebellious. It can be likened to that of a slave-owner mindset in which the slave owners did not want their slaves to become enlightened or question the status quo, but to instead, align themselves to the preestablished roles and tasks that the slave masters had established for them. The husband is not a slave owner, hanging on dearly to his "slave" and afraid that she might become too enlightened and no longer cater to his every whim and desire. Instead, he should elevate his wife to the status she deserves, as the queen in his life, and treat her as such.

Furthermore, our role in the family unit should not to be about competing for authority or position or bragging about who is in charge or who calls the shot; none of the partners is inferior to the other. The wife ought to honor and respect her husband, and the husband should also love and respect his wife—respect should flow both ways, not just one person getting all the respect and not reciprocating, which creates an imbalance.

However, the devil has deceived spouses into entering into a power struggle about who is, who ought, and who is not to be in charge. And while they are fighting that battle, the original intent that God had for us—to be fruitful, multiply, replenish, subdue, and have dominion—has been neglected. So instead of cheering each other to greatness and teaming up to make the burden lighter for each other and serve as a support system for each other, we have been reduced to playing the power tussle over who is the boss or who is in control. If we have the understanding that we are a team and we are not inferior to each other, then we would naturally respect and honor each other and would be able to submit to each other in the fear of God.

In the marriage relationship, both parties deserve to be respected; marriage is not a license to be disrespectful to each other. In essence, I have come to believe that respect is not a privilege but the right of everyone. Moreover, it should be even more important in a marriage relationship.

Some of the mentalities and attitudes addressed in this book were learned and emulated from our parents, which we adopted and believed to be good and normative. Thus, this mindset of servitude and oppression towards the wife is continuously perpetuated from one generation to the next. Even for a number of husbands who do not treat their wives like "handmaiden wives" and are actively engaged with their wives and help them, some of these men have at some point been scorned by other men and sometimes even by other women or by their mothers. They have been called "sissies" that are being controlled by their wives. And some men, even though they might be willing to help and engage more with their wives, shy away completely from doing that or do not help when around other people for fear of being seen as weaklings under their wives' control, especially if they do not have a mind of their own.

Sadly, some mothers perpetuate this mindset in their sons by giving them a pass so they do not need to meet their responsibilities or do their household chores because they are boys; instead, they engage their daughters and themselves. So the boys become men and expect their wives to take on the role of "pseudo mum" and continue the nurturing from where their mothers left off. So the wife (helper) takes on the additional role of "mother," when she was meant to be a wife—not wife-mother. Some of these mothers will even go into competition with their daughters-in-law because they feel these wives are not taking good care of their sons; these mothers sometime want to take over from them and continue pampering their sons. Such intrusion into their children's homes become a tug of war with their daughters-in-law, especially when their sons do not make an appropriate distinction between their mothers and their wives. Sadly, many women treat their husbands like they are their sons and not like adult men; so their husbands end up acting like sons that need to be guided and told what to do.

Some older generation couples did not know any better, so they could not do better; but in this generation, we know better (this book is an eye opener for you), and we ought to do better because we are without excuse.

If you are a husband and your wife already has the "queen-wife" status, and you are already helping her, being a team player, taking care of her, encouraging her, supporting her, cherishing and loving her, please keep it up. Husbands like you are rare, and you are valued. However, if your wife has not attained the "queen-wife" status, go ahead and start; it is never too late. She is counting on you.

Lastly to all the couples, I have an exercise I would like each of you to do on your own. Here are two questions I would like you to answer:

1. Which status describes you or your wife, "Queen wife" or "Handmaiden wife"?

    Answer:_____

2. Which one describes you or your husband, "King" or "Manservant"?

    Answer:_____

Now, compare each others answers. You just might be shocked that what you think is different from your spouse's reality.

Acknowledgments

To God who keeps tugging at my heart to fulfill destiny and be all he has created me to be

To my husband (King Philip) with whom I have learned and keep learning how to be a queen; I love you and appreciate you.

My girls (Ogechuka, Kachiku, and Chizite), who make me continue to aspire toward building a great legacy they can be proud of; I love you girls so much.

To my queen mum (Pastor Oby Enuma), who keeps believing that I would be all God has ordained me to be; I am eternally grateful, and I love you dearly.

To my dearest king dad (Bishop Kanayo Enuma), who kept hoping for me; I promise I will be a fulfillment of that hope; I love you and miss you so much.

To my siblings (Chichi, Amy, Ugo and Chidinma); you are the best, thanks for loving and truly supporting me; I love you guys so much.

To all my family, friends, church family, and well-wishers (I cannot name you all, but you know yourselves); thanks for your constant support and encouragement and for wishing me the best; I love and appreciate you all a whole lot.

To Bishop T. D. Jakes (my mentor) who keeps on calling out the giant in me (including this book), with his challenging, empowering, and motivating messages; I salute you, Sir.

To my pastors: Dr. Shola and AP Lola Awobajo; thanks for watching over the flocks God has committed into your hands; God will continue to honor and reward you.

To my book editor (Ed Shewan); thanks for your patience and for putting structure and order to my book; awesome job!

To all the men of God, whose names I cannot all mention but whose messages have impacted my life in one way or another; keep feeding the flock; you will never lose your reward; God has your back.

Notes

Notes

www.ingramcontent.com/pod-product-compliance
Lightning Source LLC
Chambersburg PA
CBHW032122280326
41933CB00009B/946